HAL•LEONARD
INSTRUMENTAL
PLAY-ALONG

VIOLA

Worship Favorites

CONTENTS

HOW TO USE THE CD ACCOMPANIMENT:

THE CD IS PLAYABLE ON ANY CD PLAYER, AND IS ALSO ENHANCED SO MAC AND PC USERS CAN ADJUST THE RECORDING TO ANY TEMPO WITHOUT CHANGING THE PITCH.

A MELODY CUE APPEARS ON THE RIGHT CHANNEL ONLY. IF YOUR CD PLAYER HAS A BALANCE ADJUSTMENT, YOU CAN ADJUST THE VOLUME OF THE MELODY BY TURNING DOWN THE RIGHT CHANNEL.

ISBN 978-1-4234-9937-4

HAL•LEONARD®
CORPORATION
7777 W. BLUEMOUND RD. P.O. BOX 13819 MILWAUKEE, WI 53213

Visit Hal Leonard Online at
www.halleonard.com

AGNUS DEI

Words and Music by
MICHAEL W. SMITH

VIOLA

Worshipfully

❷ EVERLASTING GOD

VIOLA

Words and Music by BRENTON BROWN
and KEN RILEY

Moderate Rock

❸ GREAT IS THE LORD

VIOLA

Words and Music by MICHAEL W. SMITH
and DEBORAH D. SMITH

Moderately Fast

◆ HE IS EXALTED

VIOLA

Words and Music by
TWILA PARIS

◆⁵ HERE I AM TO WORSHIP

VIOLA

Words and Music by
TIM HUGHES

HOSANNA
(Praise Is Rising)

VIOLA

Words and Music by PAUL BALOCHE
and BRENTON BROWN

With a driving beat

HOW MAJESTIC IS YOUR NAME

VIOLA

Words and Music by
MICHAEL W. SMITH

IN CHRIST ALONE

VIOLA

Words and Music by KEITH GETTY
and STUART TOWNEND

⑨ INDESCRIBABLE

VIOLA

Words and Music by LAURA STORY
and JESSE REEVES

10 LEAD ME TO THE CROSS

VIOLA

Words and Music by
BROOKE FRASER

MIGHTY TO SAVE

VIOLA

Words and Music by BEN FIELDING
and REUBEN MORGAN

With praise

THE POWER OF THE CROSS
(Oh to See the Dawn)

VIOLA

Words and Music by KEITH GETTY
and STUART TOWNEND

molto rit.

⟨13⟩ STILL

VIOLA

Words and Music by
REUBEN MORGAN

With reverence

◆14 THERE IS A REDEEMER

Words and Music by
MELODY GREEN

VIOLA

THE WONDERFUL CROSS

VIOLA

Words and Music by JESSE REEVES,
CHRIS TOMLIN and J. D. WALT